CW00779824

CRACKED BUT NOT BROKEN

Colin Worthington

MINERVA PRESS
MONTREUX LONDON WASHINGTON

CRACKED BUT NOT BROKEN

ISBN 1 85863 938 7

First Published 1997 by
MINERVA PRESS
195 Knightsbridge
London SW7 1RE

Printed in Great Britain by
B.W.D. Ltd, Northolt, Middlesex

CRACKED BUT NOT BROKEN

Dedicated to Fiona Gallagher

Contents

This book could not have been possible if I had never come across the exciting uninhibited work of poet and writer Leonard Cohen, which has given me many years of pleasure since the early sixties. His poetry influenced me in many ways and gave me confidence to create the style of writing to which I have now become accustomed.

Some of the most wonderful lines I've had the pleasure to digest come from such masterpieces as 'Chelsea Hotel', 'Famous Blue Raincoat', 'Suzanne', 'Closing Time', and for me his *pièce de résistance* 'First We Take Manhattan'. These classics span a period of thirty years - thirty precious years that are everlasting in the countless memories that I associate with his writing.

I will never have either the talent or the charisma of the master to even attempt to emulate his genius. I have merely tried to pen together some of my own personal thoughts and feelings. Hopefully, no one will feel offended by them, but if so, I add my humble apologies in advance.

So thanks for the memories Mr Cohen.

Colin Worthington

For Fiona

Suffering through your constant pain and
Months of discomfort
That caused changes
From deep inside
Then another kind of pain
When I betrayed you
And our love died…
My eyes were darkened cavities
And my mind possessed, unable to
See
Or think clearly enough
To realise the ultimate mistake
I was creating as I hid behind
My darkened hood
Had I listened to your plea
Without rejecting your affection
And reached out to hold you again
I would not have needed this
Second chance that I've
Received
Although having learned from
This lesson I've been taught
My eyes will always see and know
Your real pain

The Sparrow

With weary wing and throbbing breast
The sparrow plunged from the sky
Fluttering between grey concrete needles
Like a butterfly in flight
To find her place of rest on
The sidewalk deep below
Her cry of help was distanced
By the echoes of the bustling street
As she raised her tiny head in despair
Giants danced and ogres pranced around
Till gently lifted in Liberty's outstretched hand
That bathed and stroked life into her again
Clasped in that palm of freedom then
Released back to her throne
Continuing the journey high above
Through New York city skies.

New Sparrow for Bosnia

With weary wing and throbbing breast
the sparrow plunged from the sky
fluttering between grey concrete needles
like a butterfly in flight to find
her place of rest on the blood red
streets of fear below
her cry of help distanced by the
thunderous echoes of war
as she raised her tiny head in despair
giants danced and ogres pranced around
till gently lifted in the outstretched
hand of liberation that bathed then
stroked new life into her again
then released with pride from the palm
of freedom to continue her journey
of hope through the clear blue cloudless skies.

Emptiness

The longing strains when unable to give
Watching from a far removed place
Hate betrays itself when there's
Nothing left to hate… crying
Till your eyes have run dry
Night becomes day in confusion
Time turns into endless torment
Hidden
Deep inside an open wound
Festering till the pain becomes
Relief
Fighting back the hurt
That rejects itself
As a shadow closes over the
Emptiness
That creates an emptiness within
And the void becomes complete.

Crag

Rough craggy rock spans my window
Old houses separate crag from green-lined walls
As the rain begins its gentle flow
Lady cat starts her evening call

Submitting sky fills up cold grey
Sudden darkness starts to surround
While we await the dawning of a new day
When once again crag's colours will change around

Stood proud a million years or more
A sentinel watching over us all
Which once threw out fire from its core
Lady cat outside ends her evening call.

Pity

She said, "I know you from the past
Or from some other place
You played the saxophone."
I shrugged
"You blew my blues away
Whatever you say," said I
She took me in her hand
"Hey! You're not the sax man
My mistake," she said
"Pity," said I

Changes

Take a long look
Judge for yourself
Yes...
Your appearance has changed
Like the cover of a book
Which was once torn
Then rebound
Engraved
In gold leaf
And presented to you
Images
Altering like the weather
Inconsistently
Trying not to falter
Take another long gaze
You've repainted the
Exterior
Towards a new phase
Your interior remains
Unchanged
With only yourself to blame

See What You See

You only see what you want to see
Not me…
You don't see the cold grey cloud
Only me
You don't see my crazy mind
Or what I hide behind
You only see what you want to see
Not me…
You don't see my hidden gun
Only me
You don't see the broken hand
Or my tortured land
You only see what you want to see
Not me…
You don't see my infected wound
Only me
You don't see the shadow black
Or my crooked back
You only see what you want to see
Not me…
You don't see the mortal sin
Or my jagged fin
You only see what you want to see
Not me…

Pull Together

Tighten your grip boys, feel that rope taut
All eyes focussed on the quivering knot
Hear the crowd shout the ever-urging call
Dig your heels in to prevent the fall
Pull then tug, try to balance the weight
All for one now, mate for mate.
Tighten still, boys, don't give away slack
Solid steel anchorman digs in at the back
Strain then pain, hands running red
Beads of sweat dripping from your head
Dig in deeper, clear that line
Feel the give, the tell-tale sign
One more pull, joint effort, everyone
Grunts and groans pull that ton
Got them reeling on the way down
Final tug and we will wear that crown
End of day we have stood our ground
Hands are shaken, congratulations all round
Our first victory tastes oh so sweet
We're now the boys they want to beat
We may not succeed this time next year
But on this day we all cried a joyful tear.

Joy of You

You took away the fireside glow
As you knelt close by my side
I slowly touched your leg, your thigh
You trembled then you cried.
I thought of Lisbon in the spring
As you lay down next to me
I touched your lips with my hand
You smiled that smile of glee.
We moved in time side by side
You came the way you do
Then laying your hand upon my chest
You promised to be true.
I rose and left late at night
Homeward bound once more
Walking through the gentle rain
With another wondrous woman to explore.

Travelling Song

Carnival lights cascade through the night
Kaleidoscoping the cloud-filled sky
Creating shapes that drift slowly out of sight
Fading away to disappear and die

Caravans pulled by the aged beasts
Wind howling through leafless trees
Somewhere another plot to lease
Another band of children to please

Canvas raised once more from the ground
Balloons flags and streamers fly
Wooden horses travel round and round
Prizes to win, goodies to buy

Canvas lowered one more time
Hustle, bustle, move along
Listen hear the haunting rhyme
Singing the forever lingering song.

Cul-de-sac

I witnessed the making of *Cul-de-sac*
From a far off hidden place
Location was Lindisfarne –
Holy Island to some.
Directed by Polanski
Such a small man I remember
A psychological thriller
With Donald Pleasance and Lionel Stander
In leading roles
But my most exciting memory was
Catching a glimpse, such a small glimpse
Of Françoise Dorleac's wonderful
Naked breasts
Yes
I remember *Cul-de-sac* so well.

Someone Did

Don't mention it – you didn't cry
someone did
you didn't laugh
someone did
you didn't write
someone did
you didn't forgive
someone did
you didn't dance
someone did
who cares?
someone did...

Faceless

Left in turmoil from those horrendous years
Spent alone watching the darting fireside flames
Cradling inside all your hidden fears

Of not knowing when or what
To expect through the pine stained door
Or who he has brought

Home to your room, your unmade bed
Welcoming the stranger
That you know he has paid

Pitying yourself in tense anger
That dare not show its face
Which hides in the shadow of the stranger

Who has once again raped your pride
And left you faceless again
Without the chance to hide

Maybe tomorrow it will not rain
And the sky may clear its clouds.

Vision

A vision
Came to me last night
I saw
A land so far
Yet
So near
I could reach and touch
And sense
The atmosphere
And I could breathe
The air
Pure
I heard the water run
From the hillside stream
And saw tree top villages
Where animals lived
Side by side
Man was nowhere to be seen
The sky was cloudless
And peace reigned
Among all.
No war and no crime
Harmony
Being the creatures'
Rule
Fish swam free
And buffalo roamed

Wherever
Flowers grew
And withered not.
This vision remains
And no man to be seen
In this land
So far
Yet
So near.

Time

Sixty seconds
One minute
Gone
Forever

Fifty-nine minutes later
One hour
Gone
Forever

Twenty-four hours
One day
Gone
Forever

Seven days
One week
Gone
Forever

Thirty days
Cold winter's month
Gone
Forever

Another new year
Of poverty
Stays
Forever

Coffee Time

Bliss
Coffee time in the morning
After a night of red wine
Smell that smell
Taste that taste
Coffee time in the morning
After a night of red wine
Mecca!

Control

I sleep
I dream
Without control
Who pulls my strings?
Who gave me wings that made me fly?
I soar
I dive
Without control
Who pulls my strings?
Who gave me tears so I could cry?
I talk
I speak
Without control
Who pulls my strings?
Who gave me words so I could lie?
I know
I think
Without control
Who pulls my strings?
Who gave me thought to wonder why?
I grow
I age
Without control
Who pulls my strings?
Who gave me life to let me die?

The Window

The island grew cold and grey
As winter approached
The loneliness remained
Intact
A blanket, a book, and
A cat for comfort
By the fireside bright
Once again I hear a tap on
The window
That dreaded curse has
Returned
And leaves me helpless
As it enters
And feeds its hunger
On me
Satisfied
It leaves back through
The window
And I am left
Drained
Feeling only pain
Anger and
Hate
Once again
Till the next time.

Solitary

The voice touched a deep shade of blue
But no one really listened
As a shadow slowly engulfed
The words
The silence became the reality
Till the hunter raised its head
Absorbing all
That anticipated the return
Of the enigma
Towards another decade of
Solitude
Till once again we will hear
And feel
That deeper shade of blue.

Classic Line

Most films produce at least one
Memorable line
Whether its said by Bogart, Cagney
Or whoever
Some of these films remain forgotten
But those wonderful lines - never

Secret

A secret was told
Many years ago
And not a word was said
No matter what
Or who
Passed my way
I remained loyal
I remained true
Then our friendship
Broke
And so did my tongue
Sorry.

Amongst

I've stood amongst men
Whom I knew not
Friends and enemies
Alike
What do I know?
Thieves
Muggers
Fraudsters
Bigamists
Rapists
Sadists
Cheats
Wife-beaters
Arsonists
Child-molesters
Psychopaths
Murderers
Conservatives

Statistics tell me I will know or talk
With at least one person in each of the
Above categories, in my lifetime

Surely not!
I could never visualise myself
Conversing with a
Conservative

But what do I know?

Taken

I was taken
By you
With your words your books
Your lust
Your revenge was taken
On me
I became your victim
Your puppet.
I became your punishment
Your guilt
I laid down to your slavery
Your chains and straps
And rouge.
I became red or blue for you
Whatever the mood
Executioner or prisoner
Masochist
Sadist
Lover or hater
Or both.
I became leather
Then silk
Whatever your skins desire
Your ecstasy
Your nightmare
Your burden
Then I became free.

Faither

A dark shadow has cast across the room
As the days had become much too long
And the sun eclipsed behind the moon
When this gentleman sadly moved on
The game will never ever be the same
There will be something not quite right
Everything now all seems oh so tame
Someone is missing on a Thursday night
Some men come and some men go
Some play serious, some just for fun
But none had that special special flow
Like Faither potting into bag one
Our thoughts can never be erased
Whatever happens whatever may come
They can even take away the green baize
But our memories of Faither cannot be undone.

Hero

You walk the clouds
On your golden shoes
Floating
Through the calm
Like a prince on a white
Charger
Working towards your
New day
Which you enter in a
Proud majestic way
That leaves all in your
Wake.
Presenting yourself in the
Total freedom
That runs through your
Veins
That gives you the will
To be.
Your solidity strives
Through the backbone
Of your soul
In complete fulfilment
Of your inner self
As the aura surrounds you
For all to see.

Forever Green

The rapturous roar will soon end
and a ghostly silence will leave
an emptiness over the hallowed
green
where thousands have openly wept
at the glory and pride which has
given so much pleasure for a
century and more
from cloth cap to reversed baseball
hat
from Reilly through to Wright
icons of our youth
heroes of our dreams
cannot be replaced by concreting
this precious land
we will always hear the echoes in the wind
and feel the ecstasy felt by all
when the glory, glory boys entered that arena
causing the spine to tingle and eyes
to swell with unashamed tears of emotion
and pride
yes, they can take away the stadium
and close the gates of heaven forever
but replace Hibernian – never

Physio

I lift
I turn
I twist
I stretch
I bend
I push
I cycle
I pull
I climb
I hold
I arch
I sweat
I ache
I rest
I repeat
And repeat
And repeat
And ache.

PMR Physiotherapy 1994

Shadow

Sometimes dark
Sometimes tall
Sometimes at my back
Then to the fore
Distorted
It climbs the wall
Changing shape as it
Reaches the ceiling
And darts across the room
Disappearing through the
Window
To rest upon the wall
Opposite
Only to return
As I turn
It follows
Crouching
As I sit
Becoming
A shapeless mass
As it falls under my feet
Re-emerging
As I rise
Turning out the light

It loses all
Lying still
Through the night
Awaiting
Another summer's day.

Touch

If I could touch your silk with my lips
And crease you not
Or brush the silver plait that
Flows down your back
I would re-welcome.
If I could velvet your heart
I would re-enter
Or shine buttercup under your chin –
Only... petals crumble in time.
If my sun could reach your darkness
Your light would surely flicker
Never again to dim.
If my music could make you dance
Your soul to return
Replacing
The cripple within.

Stalked

He stalks on the open weakness
Feeding on the fear
That claws and rips
When all else has failed
Sneering at your wishful hopes
From deep inside
Grinning
As all is to be revealed
Knocking
On your locked door
Wearing that grotesque mask
Now that you are finally unveiled
Gnawing
At the walls of the canyon
That carry your river
Towards the sea
That again is longing to be sailed
You search your mind's control
Which creates an Everest
To ascend
Like has never before been scaled
Then you soar like an eagle
To turn aside this Satan...
Your victory
Raises its glorious head
And once again
This cancerous parasite has been nailed.

Beyond

On high ground
The sacred burial mound
Stretches
Towards
The great bear
And
Beyond
The moon
To leave behind
The pine
The arrow
The wigwam
The totem
And the river
Which once turned
Red
From our fathers'
Blood
Travelling further
And further
From
The near genocide
Towards
The land of peace
And
Our eternal Manitou

Cusp

A raging bull
Or heavenly twin
Am I one?
Or both?
Could I be
Neither?
Or either?
In reverse
Position
Perhaps
This explains
My personality
Change
And indecision
Or
Is this an appropriate
Excuse
I use
Let's see
Tonight I may decide
To be a bit of
One
Or the other
Then again
Maybe not...

Bottle

Sinking deeper in pure wallow
Drowning
Forgetting the tomorrow
The consequences.
The ugliness becomes the beauty
Joining
Together in unity
Total blindness.
1989 classic red
Smooth
Searching through your head
Absorbing.
Now somewhat a reveller
Loudly
Producing this leveller
Courageously
Words flow in ease
Repetitively
Inhibitions cease
In inspiration.
The bottle may be drained
But
The mind is now full.

Island

Paul Brady sang of the island
Tracing your footsteps in the sand
I want to go further
And feel your palm in my hand

To hear the breeze brushing by
Children's castles in the sky
I want to see again
The tears run from your eye

To absorb this summer's day
And hear the words you used to say
I want to be with you
Looking over this special bay

To touch the moon late at night
Casting shadows through the light
Feeling your closeness
And watching this wondrous sight

To soar above the water's flow
That holds secrets we will never know
As we lie together
And our bodies gently move to and fro.

Paul Brady sang of the island
Tracing your footsteps in the sand
I want to go further
And leave my spirit within this land.

Hunt

The cry was loud and oh so clear –
Tally-ho! Followed by the shrilling horn,
Bush-tailed prey the reluctant pawn,
Carnivorous fiends lead the scarlet red

Across fields of blood the victim ran.
Rigid horsemen sit pompously tight
Chasing pack hunts the first bite:
A gentleman's sport, the gentleman said

Hounds from hell chasing the game,
Lady fox zigzags in total fear,
Saliva dripping from those getting near
Starving bellies soon to be fed.

Caught by the throat and torn apart
One against twenty in utter fury
Man is the judge, the hounds are the jury
Passing the sentence far above God's head

Howls of victory end the bloody day;
Lords of the manor sitting so proud
Welcomed home by the cheering crowd.
Alas! The true beast is the one not dead.

Disciple

I followed the master
And his fortunes
From Montreal to Hydra
And back
From Suzanne and Marianne
And those Sisters of Mercy
Who became
Teachers
And told us Stories from the Streets
I survived
Along with you
And a bunch of Lonesome Heroes
To seek out
A Partisan of the Old Revolution
Then Joan of Arc
Re-emerged
Through an Avalanche
Of Love and Hate
Returning
To the Chelsea Hotel
Which you remember so well
But you got away, didn't you,
To leave a woman waiting
With only Memories?
As this lost Canadian
Entertained The Guests which
Included sweet Jennifer

And The Gypsy's Wife
Who Danced to the End of Love
Before
Coming back to you
And I cannot forget how
The Jazz Police
First took Manhattan
Then
Waited for the miracle
Of
The Future
To sail on through
The Democracy
Always
Trying to be for real
Till Closing Time
Yes
I remember it well
From Montreal to Hydra
And back...

Barriers

The barrier rose both slowly and unwillingly
Like a self-imposed inner scream
As we ambled along hopefully.
Take twenty-five from a film scene
Monumental stumbling blocks readily erected
Built high on high
Fenced in and openly protected
Shackled… no matter how you try.
An obstacle of silence to overcome
Brick by brick removing the wall
Picking the pieces crumb by crumb
To finally hear that silent call.

C.A.B. Blues
(The Dundas Street Shuffle)

Another wet dismal morning to cherish and fulfil;
I've even remembered my high blood pressure pill.
Once again the waiting-room is filled almost to the brim
"Next client, please" - oh no, surely it's not him.

"Good morning, sir, and how are we today?"
Remember, listen carefully to what he has to say.
"Now sit yourself right down there" (while I get near the door)
"Yes, I see, I see" (God, there's more and more and more).

"What was that? Tomorrow you're due back up in court?
Yes, I will work out your claim regarding Income Support.
No! First of all, you need to complete this form.
I wonder which one of us will end up in a hospital dorm?"

"Now then, Family Credit, those dreaded calculations again
And noisy neighbours 'wi nae peace in yer ain hame'
Five children and one on the way, maybe two
Here we go again, 'Aye, son, it's awright for you.'"

"Invalidity?" God, now he thinks he's disabled.
Under which file will this lot be labelled?
"Oh, you have trouble getting home from the pub most nights.
Yes, sir, after all, you *are* entitled to your rights."

“What’s that? There’s *more*? A matter of some debt
The bookie won’t pay out on your winning bet?”
I wonder why I even bothered to ask,
My kingdom for a coffee, oh my kingdom for that flask.

“Your next client’s awaiting, something about a lease
Please make it simple and give me some peace
The old lady in the corner - yes, that one over there.”
“Hello, there, madam. Oh no! *Please*, no, not her!

The Apocalypse Four

Walking hand in hand towards the sea
Having had our fill of deep red wine,
Fiona, Sandra, Raymond and me
Hand in hand, four in a line

Bravely ignoring the cold and the fears,
Golden sand running through our toes
Water closing in on these four musketeers
Soon to be in saturated clothes.

Such crazy fun had by one and all
Now wading deeper in Indian file
Watching carefully not to trip or fall
Helping Fiona's fears disappear for a while

On and on ride the Apocalypse Four
Returning home to drink some more...

Un-Named

There was no prisoner to capture along the way.
The hope and faith had long been deserted
With no sorrow to numb your mind.

Where was the wisdom and where was the truth
That used to linger from each thought
Before the skies became a dome of fire

Of mortar primed from either side of the river
Casting splintered shadows on the water below.
Is there no longer the gift of knowledge?

Only another life to sever
As there was no prisoner to capture along the way.

Keep

Cobbled stone street
Stretch a royal mile
(Reach) towards
The rocky castle keep

Where history dwells
In dungeon deep below
(Hold) secrets
Among the spiders creep

Broken lock and rusty chain
Lie dormant
(Forever) concealing
The horror and shame

Medieval days now long gone
Victims cut free
(Today) begging
A shilling for a song

This monument of days passed by
Withhold the truth within.

Obtrusive

Scaffolds clang and bricks hammer
Into shape
Loud shouts from mate to mate
Above the drone of a drill
Mechanical
Monumental crane swings to and fro
Across my head
Shrilling whistle blows from afar
Luxurious peace
For an hour or so
Sound of sawing wood a distance away
Signals the return
Voices
Bellow instruction
To these men of construction
Who sweat
Till suits arrive standing firm
And point
Nodding their ill-fitted safety helmeted heads
Yellow
Alas... My forever changeant crag will soon be
Shadowed
Concrete
Grey.

Question

A question was asked many years ago
But there was only a muted answer.
Who can control this eternal flow?
"I," cried the Egyptian dancer

Rushing on a high and plunging to a low
White as a dove but black as a crow.

A question was asked many years ago
When a new-born babe was born,
An arrow was released from its bow
Encircled in a ring of thorn,

Rushing on a high and plunging to a low
White as a dove but black as a crow.

A question was asked many years ago
And is heard almost every day
Surrounded by a haloed glow
Lighting a candle to show the way

But we still worship the calf of gold
And ski on the mound of snow

'Cane

The dawn broke like any normal morning
And the sun peered through thick cotton cloud.
Light breeze started to howl without warning
Becoming stronger and deafeningly loud.

Creatures ran and hid in fear
Sheltering where they could find.
Twisting needle closing in so near
Confused and running blind.

The dreaded 'cane cracking all in its midst;
Trees, steeples, and houses lay flat.
Striking home like a tight clenched fist
Wind shrilling like a demented rat.

Catastrophe brought about by nature's call
Leaving total destruction in its wake.
Trees snapped like a broken doll,
Fields swollen like a great lake.

Calm returns in eerie silence
Everyone stunned and everything shaken.
Rebuild the wall and fix the fence
Hoping this 'cane will never re-awaken.

The Lost Seasons

Seasons four we at one time had
In this our lovely native land:
Spring flowers and new lambs born;
Blue summer skies with sun all day long;
Autumn breezes brought falling leaves;
Winter skating on ponds that did freeze.
Whatever happened to our seasons four?
I've searched but can find no more
Except for a few days here and there
Just enough to let us compare
Between them.
When our year was once divided
And now when the weather is so undecided
Where, oh where, did they go?
The four seasons that we once loved so.

Jane (Jean) Worthington, 1962